A BIBLE STUDY BY MARTHA THATCHER

WHEN THE SQUEEZE IS ON

NAVPR

A MINISTRY OF T   ʌATORS
P.O. BOX 35001, COLORADO SPRINGS, COLORADO 80935

The Navigators is an international Christian
organization. Jesus Christ gave His follow-
ers the Great Commission to go and make
disciples (Matthew 28:19). The aim of The
Navigators is to help fulfill that commission by
multiplying laborers for Christ in every nation.

NavPress is the publishing ministry of The
Navigators. NavPress publications are tools
to help Christians grow. Although publications alone cannot make disciples or change
lives, they can help believers learn biblical
discipleship, and apply what they learn to their
lives and ministries.

Eighth printing, 1994

Printed in the United States of America.

Contents

Author

Martha Thatcher and her husband, Brian, are on staff with The Navigators in Dana Point, California. Martha is a graduate of Barrington College. She and Brian have three children.

Martha is a freelance author and conference speaker. She is also working toward a Master's of Science in Nursing.

Before You Begin

We have all felt the squeeze of pressure. Sometimes it's a vice-like grip that pushes us to the border of panic. But most of the time it's an annoying hold that can drain our energy and sap our joy. The everyday elements of life can crowd in and threaten to overwhelm us.

Handling your pressures biblically is a tough job. But it *is* possible. As you work through this study, you will not discover easy answers and one-step solutions to the complicated maze of your individual pressures. But you *will* develop in your ability to think biblically, and to draw applicable principles from the Scriptures concerning pressure areas. You will also have many opportunities to apply those principles to your own situation in realistic and manageable steps.

God is interested in helping us move forward from where we are. But we are all different. As a result, you will benefit most not from finding "right" answers, but from your thoughtful observations.

You can use this study alone or in a group. Its design will allow it to fit well into any group setting—among men and women at work, in church, or at home. It's important for each group member to prepare his or her study faithfully, because it is primarily in this individual study that we open ourselves up to God's work in changing our lives. The group setting then provides an opportunity for mutual ministry and encouragement as each person shares from the richness of his or her personal study.

Each chapter has ten questions, giving you these advantages:

- If preparation time and/or discussion time is limited, each lesson is easily divided in half.
- You can divide your preparation time into five segments and prepare two questions each day during the week. (Although taking an hour or an hour-and-a-half at one time to prepare each lesson is desirable, many of us wouldn't do any study at all if we had to rely on such large blocks of time.)

As you work through *When the Squeeze Is On*, ask God to help you not only learn His truth, but also work out His truth in your daily life. The value and impact of what God teaches you will be greater if you memorize the Bible verses that you find most meaningful to your situation.

Expect God to begin a fresh work in your life as you study and apply His living Word.

> *The law of the LORD is perfect,*
> *reviving the soul.*
> *The statutes of the LORD are trustworthy,*
> *making wise the simple.*
> *The precepts of the LORD are right,*
> *giving joy to the heart.*
> *The commands of the LORD are radiant,*
> *giving light to the eyes. . . .*
> *May the words of my mouth and the meditation*
> *of my heart*
> *be pleasing in your sight,*
> *O LORD, my Rock and My Redeemer.*
>   (Psalm 19:7-8,14)

CHAPTER ONE

HERE COMES PRESSURE!

Pressure may be actual or merely perceived. In either case, it is experienced as real. As we seek to deal biblically with our experiences of pressure, and as we encourage others to do the same, it will help to understand some of the dynamics involved.

> What is pressure?
> Where does it come from?
> What contributes to it?
> What effects does it have?

WHAT IS PRESSURE?

1. How would you define pressure? You may prefer to use the definition you find in a dictionary.

In itself, pressure is neither good nor bad; it is neutral.

> We can often experience a sense of pressure and not be able to pinpoint its source correctly or, perhaps, at all. When we understand the starting point of a given pressure, we are often better able to deal with it well.

2. Pressure is not a twentieth-century phenomenon. Our pressures today arise from the same types of situations that produced pressure for biblical characters.

a. Keeping your definition in mind, examine the following passages. Describe where pressure was coming from, and what feelings may have resulted.

WHAT PRODUCED PRESSURE	POSSIBLE FEELINGS
Joseph (Genesis 37:3-8,18) Family relationships; his brothers hated him.	Lonely, fearful, hurt (angry?)
Joseph (Genesis 39:5-20)	
The Israelites (Exodus 1:8-14,22)	

WHAT PRODUCED PRESSURE	POSSIBLE FEELINGS
Martha (Luke 10:38-40)	

b. Look over what you recorded in the chart. As you reflect on your own acquaintance with pressure, underline the feelings and types of situations that you can identify with.

c. The causes of pressure are countless. Think of one or two sources of pressure in addition to the ones listed above. Be as specific as possible.

3. Read 2 Chronicles 20:1-12. Jehoshaphat, king of Judah, was facing double pressure, as we all do often.

a. What situation was creating major pressure?

b. Verse 12 records that Jehoshaphat didn't know what to do. His uncertainty, added to the original pressure, created double pressure. Briefly describe a situation in which you experienced this two-fold pressure.

c. In the midst of this overwhelming circumstance, what did Jehoshaphat do? (Also see Psalm 25:15.)

d. How could you follow Jehoshaphat's example the next time you face double pressure?

WHAT CONTRIBUTES TO PRESSURE?
---

4. Many of life's pressures are out of our control. However, we do sometimes create our own pressure. And sometimes we add to existing pressure unnecessarily. Study the following verses to determine in what ways the people involved created, or contributed to, their own pressure.

David (Psalm 32:3-5)

The disciples (John 15:18-21)

Moses (Hebrews 11:24-25)

James's readers (James 4:1-2)

Optional
From your study of the verses in question 4, identify which pressures resulted from following God (✓) and which ones didn't (×).

---

5. Judges 16:16 tells us that Samson was under pressure: "He was tired to death" of Delilah's nagging. Read Judges 16:4-21 and use your observations from the passage to answer the following questions:

   a. What was Delilah pressing Samson about?

   b. How many times is her question (and subsequent action) recorded?

   c. Verses 19-21 record the cruel outcome of the situation. Do you think Samson was a victim? Why or why not?

   d. What comment does Proverbs 22:3 make on the passage you just read?

e. Think of a question to ask yourself, when you are under pressure, that will help you decide if you are following Samson's example.

Creating such a question is no easy task. However, if we can make a habit of turning biblical truth into questions we ask ourselves and try to answer honestly, we will have a significant tool for God to use in changing us for the better.

WHAT EFFECTS DOES PRESSURE HAVE?

6. Jezebel, wife of King Ahab, put severe pressure on the prophet Elijah; she threatened to kill him. Read 1 Kings 19:1-18 and answer the following questions to examine the effect this intense pressure had on Elijah.

a. How did he feel and react after Jezebel's threat?

b. How did these feelings and actions compare with his emotions and behavior the day before? (See 1 Kings 18:18,21,27,40.)

c. Contrast Elijah's perception of reality with what was true.

d. Compare what Elijah wanted to do next with what God wanted him to do next.

7. a. Based on your study of Elijah's situation, comment on the effect pressure can have on

our feelings.

our perspective of reality.

our intentions and subsequent actions.

b. Fill in this "effect line" by deciding in which order, from your perspective, the three areas above are affected by pressure.

————————→ affect(s) —————————→ which then ———————————.
                                                        affect(s)

8. Our values are often hidden, even from ourselves. What seems to be true and what is true can be different. Under pressure, we sometimes learn the truth about ourselves.

In the following chart, compare what seemed to be true about the person or people with what turned out to be true, as pressure revealed it.

WHAT SEEMED TO BE TRUE	WHAT WAS TRUE
Rich Young Ruler (Matthew 19:16-22) Willing to do anything to obtain eternal life.	Unwilling to give up his riches.
Israelites (Exodus 14:31, 16:2-3)	
Peter (Mark 14:31,66-72)	

9. Sometimes pressure will reveal qualities that remain hidden under normal circumstances.

a. Describe an experience of pressure in which you were surprised (pleasantly or unpleasantly) to learn some truth about yourself.

16

b. What had you assumed to be true about yourself before this?

c. What did the pressure situation reveal to be true?

10. a. What is one of the more significant areas of pressure in your life at this time?

b. Where does it come from?

c. What is contributing to it?

d. What effect is it having on you?

Why not ask God right now to use this Bible study to help you deal with that pressure in His way?

11. What have you discovered through your study that helps you understand pressure better? How can your insight help you?

> Multiply one day's crises by 365. Add financial strain, inflation, traffic jams, unemployment, unplanned pregnancies, failure at school, obesity, smog, surgery, loneliness, alcoholism, drugs, and death. Subtract the support of the family unit. Divide by dozens of different opinions . . . and you come up with a formula that has the makings of madness.
>
> Block all avenues of escape and you have an enormous powder keg with a terribly short fuse. Even if you are a Christian . . . and love God intensely . . . and believe the Bible . . . and genuinely want to walk in obedience. . . .
>
> Christians need to be told that difficulty and pressure are par for the course. No amount of biblical input or deeper-life conferences or super-victory seminars will remove our human struggles. God promises no bubble of protection, no guaranteed release from calamity.[1]

If pressure is going to be a stimulus for growth, we must learn to face the inevitable pressures of life with both an understanding of the key issues and a practical "handle" on how to respond biblically.

NOTE: 1. Charles R. Swindoll, *Three Steps Forward, Two Steps Back* (Nashville, Tennessee: Thomas Nelson Publishers, 1980), page 14.

CHAPTER TWO

GETTING PERSPECTIVE

With pressure comes a myriad of questions:

> Should I try to "get out from under" it?
> Should I try to change anything?
> If so, what? And to what degree?
> Or should I allow it to continue, and try to manage it?
> How do I know if I'm managing it effectively?
> Is this pressure going to be good or bad for me?
> How can I know the difference?

God desires to teach us how to cut through the dynamics of pressure and learn how to handle the variety of pressures that face us.

JESUS' RESPONSE TO PRESSURE

In the sixth chapter of his gospel, John recorded the incident when Jesus fed more than five thousand people. What John did not record are the events of the approximately twenty-four hours prior to the miracle. Before turning to John 6, let's do some investigation to understand the background of the incident.

1. Read Matthew 14:6-13 and Mark 6:7-13,30-31, which

describe some of what took place prior to the miraculous feeding.

a. What were John's disciples and Jesus' disciples telling Jesus?

John's disciples

Jesus' disciples

b. Do you think that this was a time of significant pressure for Jesus? Use details from the passages to support your answer.

c. What suggestion did Jesus make to the disciples?

d. Why do you think He suggested that?

2. John 6:1-13 records the events that followed the trip across the Sea of Galilee.

a. What was Jesus doing when He saw the crowd coming?

b. If you had been in the disciples' place, what would have gone through your mind as you watched at least 5,000 people approaching? (Remember Jesus' intention in crossing the Sea of Galilee.)

c. What did the people want?

d. How did Jesus respond in attitude and action to the pressures of their presence and their need?

3. Verses 14 and 15 of John 6 describe yet another pressure on Jesus as a result of the miraculous feeding; the people wanted to make Him king "by force."

a. How did Jesus respond?

b. How did Jesus' handling of this situation differ from the way He handled the need to feed the people?

Look up the following verses and make note of the variety of
ways that Jesus interacted with pressure.

Luke 6:7-11

John 11:2-6

Philippians 2:8

4. Whenever we find ourselves under pressure, and desire to
respond purposefully (not merely *react instinctively*), we
wrestle with some or all of the questions listed at the begin-
ning of this chapter.

    a. On what basis did Jesus, who was fully human,
    decide which response was needed in each situation?

    John 4:34

    John 8:29

John 12:23-28

b. Finish the following sentence in a way that summarizes your discoveries from the verses in question 4:

Jesus knew how to respond appropriately and effectively to a variety of pressure situations because

---

YOUR RESPONSE TO PRESSURE

We respond to pressure—as to everything else—based on our personality, background, and experiences. Sometimes it's hard to identify our orientation, yet doing so will often help us understand our responses. Also, if change is needed, understanding "where we're coming from" will help us deal with the *root* of our responses. This honesty of heart pleases God.

5. The Scriptures are rich with accounts of real people and their real struggles. The people listed in the chart on the next page wrestled with issues that pressed them. Identify the pressing issue, the response of the person (or people), and the reason behind each response. The example will get you started.

THE ISSUE	THE RESPONSE	THE REASON BEHIND THE RESPONSE
Asaph (Psalm 73:12-20) Questioning God's treatment of the righteous and the wicked; it didn't seem fair.	At first, anger, resentment, and frustration. Then it changed to contentment.	At first Asaph was looking at things from a human perspective. When he got God's perspective, he changed.
Peter (Matthew 16:21-23)		
The Sadducees (Mark 12:18-24)		
Peter and John (Acts 4:18-19)		

Pressures often pile up. Or sometimes we are faced with a decision of whether or not to get involved in a situation we know will subject us to pressure. Can you think of an example?

Perhaps "everyday" stress just wears us down. Details and feelings crowd in. At such times it's difficult to get hold of a basis for knowing what to do. What is some of the everyday stress in your life?

6. We are assured, in 1 Peter 2:21, that Jesus is our example as we deal with whatever pain and pressure we may encounter in life.

a. Look over the thoughts you recorded in questions 4 and 5. Which of the people mentioned in question 5 do you think responded to their situations on the same basis as Jesus did? How can you tell?

b. How do you think you can respond to your own pressures, both routine and overwhelming, on the same basis as Jesus did?

7. a. What principles in the following verses can help you establish the same foundation Jesus had for understanding how to handle pressure?

25

Psalm 43:2-4

Proverbs 3:5-6

Romans 12:2

Ephesians 5:8,10,15-17

b. How do you think we can renew our minds and find out what pleases the Lord?

8. As Jesus responded to life—including pressure—from the perspective of God, so can we, increasingly. Examine the verses listed in the chart on page 27, looking for *practical means* by which you can grow in knowing God's perspective. Then think of a *habit* that will help you put that means to work in your life. Use the example shown to guide your thinking.

PRACTICAL MEANS	HELPFUL HABIT
Proverbs 1:23 Respond readily to God's rebuke.	If God tells me I'm wrong about something, I won't defend myself. I'll ask forgiveness and take a step within 24 hours to right the matter.
Psalm 119:16	
Psalm 119:59-60	
Matthew 6:31-33	
Luke 5:16	

9. Take a few moments to reflect on your own life. Describe your basis for responding to pressure as it compares with Jesus' basis. (It's difficult to evaluate such things, but if you ask Him to, God will use your honest effort to help you arrive at some degree of clarity.)

10. As you look back over this lesson, particularly the helpful habits listed in question 8, perhaps you can identify one specific step to take this week to be more available to learn God's perspective. List that step (maybe a habit you'll begin) and be specific about details (when, etc.).

Teach me your way, O LORD,
and I will walk in your truth;
give me an undivided heart,
that I may fear your name.
(Psalm 86:11)

CHAPTER THREE

RESPONDING EFFECTIVELY

The schedule presses. Problems demand solutions. Decisions loom. Responsibilities weigh heavily. The expectations of others run high. Energy runs low. Money runs out.

Applying God's perspective to the pressures of our lives is rarely a simple matter of finding a relevant verse and doing what it says. God calls on us to *think*. We need to examine our situation from what we know of God's perspective, then *make choices* and *adopt attitudes* that reflect Him.

RESPONDING IN CHOICES

Foundational to understanding God's perspective is a good grasp of His intentions for our lives. As we get hold of those intentions, more of His interaction with us will make sense. We'll also gain a more concrete basis from which to determine if some of the pressures we face are furthering His purposes or detracting from them.

1. As you study the following verses, what do you discover about the nature of God's intentions for your life?

Isaiah 30:18

Isaiah 46:10-11

Jeremiah 29:11

John 10:10

Galatians 5:1

2. Ephesians 4:22-24 is an "overview" passage; it does not include detailed instruction about particular issues. Instead, the Apostle Paul portrays, in broad terms, what direction God wants us to *grow* in. Paul describes a process.

   a. Identify two or three major elements of the growth process that God wants to see in your life. Then brainstorm about how you can actively contribute to growth in those elements.

ELEMENT	ACTIVE CONTRIBUTION TO GROWTH

ELEMENT	ACTIVE CONTRIBUTION TO GROWTH

b. What does John 17:17 contribute to your understanding of Ephesians 4:22-24?

c. Some pressures will *contribute to* God's intentions in our lives; for instance, the time pressure involved in having a consistent quiet time. What are one or two pressures that will further God's intentions in your life?

d. On the other hand, some pressures *hinder* His intentions. List two or three.

3. Study Philippians 2:12-13. Whose responsibility do you think it is to see that you are increasingly living according to God's intentions every day? Why do you think that?

4. Proverbs 6:1-5 is advice given to someone who finds himself under a particular pressure that is hindering God's purposes in his life, and about which he is able to make a choice. (You may not identify with this person's situation, but the lesson here is in the *effect* of the situation and the man's *response*.)

    a. List some words that indicate the hindering quality of the pressure.

    b. What is this person advised to do?

    c. How is he told to go about it?

    d. Hebrews 12:1 seems to summarize Proverbs 6:1-5. What principle is the writer of Hebrews giving us? (You may want to look up this verse in more than one version of the Bible.)

5. To summarize what you've learned about your choices under pressure, complete the following principle:

To determine whether to live with or remove a given pressure, I will

---

RESPONDING IN ATTITUDE

We do not always have the freedom to change a situation involving pressure. Some things, such as illness and accidents, are beyond our control. (When we clearly have no options in a pressure situation, we can be certain that the pressure is serving God's purposes, whether we understand them or not.)

We may discover that change is possible in a situation, but choose not to make a change because the circumstance seems to be furthering God's intentions. Can you think of an example?

In either case, our need is to get *as clear a picture as possible of what God desires to accomplish* through the pressure, and *a grasp of the attitudes we can develop* in order to cooperate with His desire.

6. The following verses and passages give us glimpses into some of God's purposes in allowing pressure to bear down on our lives. List each purpose you discover, then give an explanation of how pressure might help accomplish that purpose. (There are no wrong explanations; your thoughtful responses will reflect what God is teaching you, as an individual, right now.)

THE PURPOSE	HOW PRESSURE HELPS THE PURPOSE
Psalm 119:68-71 *That I might learn and obey God's Word.*	*Being afflicted can force me to the Word and help me see the seriousness of obeying God.*
Zechariah 3:9	
Hebrews 12:11	
James 1:2-3	
1 Peter 1:6-7	

Optional
Read Psalm 66:1-12. According to the psalmist, what is God like? How had He responded to the Israelites in their time of pressure? How do you think the psalmist's beliefs about God affected his perspective of the pressure?

7. a. As you study the scriptures in the chart below, identify attitudes and efforts that please God when you are under pressure. How might these attitudes and efforts be demonstrated in your daily life? (Use the last reference as your example, see page 36.)

ATTITUDE OR EFFORT	DEMONSTRATION
Psalm 24:4-5	
Psalm 62:8	
Hebrews 12:12-13	

ATTITUDE OR EFFORT	DEMONSTRATION
1 Peter 4:19 *Commit myself to God and keep doing good.*	*Staying responsible under pressure, looking for opportunities to do good to others; not giving up.*

b. Which attitude, effort, or demonstration do you find the most difficult to carry out under pressure?

c. Why do you think you have difficulty with this?

8. God's character never changes. Psalm 96 can help us understand some aspects of His character that will undergird us as we seek to grow in our God-pleasing responses during pressure. List the three or four aspects of God's character that you find most meaningful, then think of how those truths about Him can affect your responses.

Verse __6__ God is *powerful.*
Therefore I can *be sure He is able to work in my situation.*

Verse ____ God is
Therefore I can

Verse ____ God is
Therefore I can

Verse _____ God is
Therefore I can

God can use your discoveries from Psalm 96 in times of
pressure, to help you gain His perspective and experience
His care. Why not copy these discoveries on an index card
and keep it handy. Reading it when you are under pressure
will be an affirmation of who God is in relation to your
situation.

9. Romans 8:28 is often used to advise and attempt to com-
fort those who are in the midst of trying pressures. Yet in
Hebrews 11 we read long lists of people who trusted God
during terrible pressure without, in most cases, experiencing "good results."

   a. Read Romans 8:28 and Hebrews 11:13 and 39, then
   think over what you discovered in questions 1 through
   8. What do you think it means that God is working "for
   the good of those that love him"?

   b. How can that understanding help you face the pressures God allows in *your* life?

10. a. Look back to question 10 of chapter one. What signif-
     icant area of pressure did you identify? (If you didn't
     identify one then, do so now.)

b. Do you think the reason you are under that pressure reflects God's intentions?

If it doesn't, what will you do about it?

If it does, what attitude and/or effort do you need to work on in order to fully cooperate with God's intention in allowing the pressure?

c. What initial step can you take this week to move in the direction you described above?

Obedience to God's Word usually involves one small step, followed by another, and so on. Plan these steps as you would any other important endeavor: be specific and practical. Ask God to give you creative ideas for how to live out His truth in the particular area you are concerned about. You may want to make yourself accountable to someone so you will follow through with your plan.

I will give them singleness of heart and action,
so that they will always fear me
for their own good
and the good of their children after them.
(Jeremiah 32:39)

CHAPTER FOUR

TIME

The way we spend our time is the way we spend our lives. Is it an investment, or merely an expenditure?

In this chapter, we'll look at time from God's perspective, and at our use of the time allotted to us. Our interaction with time can be one of the major sources of pressure in our lives. As you prepare this chapter, ask God to show you which of the time pressures you experience are from Him and which are not.

1. a. What facts do the following verses reveal about time?

Genesis 1:14

Psalm 103:15

Proverbs 27:1

Ecclesiastes 8:6

b. Thinking of time as a *resource*, use your discoveries from the preceding verses to write a summary statement.

Time is a resource that

> Jesus didn't often speak specifically about time. Instead, He modeled His perspective.

2. Compare Luke 3:23 with Luke 4:40 and Luke 13:10-13. It would seem that Jesus could have helped more people if He had started younger, or lived longer, or hurried more. Yet He didn't. What do you think these glimpses reveal concerning Jesus' view of time?

3. Read Mark 5:21-43.

a. How did the urgency of the father's request (verses 22-23) influence Jesus' use of time?

b. Why do you think Jesus stopped (verse 30), considering the life-and-death situation awaiting Him, and the fact that the woman who touched Him was already healed (verses 27-29)?

c. Jesus' *beliefs* were behind His actions. Based on your observations of His actions, discern at least one thing He believed about

God's control.

how time should be used.

urgency and hurrying-up.

4. a. John 3:34 and John 17:4 reflect Jesus' primary concern. What was that concern?

   b. How might such a concern have shown itself in Jesus' "schedule"?

5. Jesus' use of time flowed from His priorities. Our use of time will flow from our priorities.

   a. According to the scriptures listed in the chart on pages 42-43, what should be your lifelong priorities?

   b. How might each priority show in your use of time?

PRIORITY	USE OF TIME
Matthew 5:16 *Shine my light;* *do good.*	*Take time to relate to non Christians.* *Be observant and plan to do good,* *even if only in small ways.*
Matthew 22:37, John 14:21	
Matthew 22:39, John 13:34	
Matthew 28:19-20	
1 Timothy 4:7-8	

PRIORITY	USE OF TIME
1 Timothy 5:8	
Colossians 3:23	

c. As you translate those lifelong priorities into the daily realities of your life, what do you think should be your top three or four daily priorities? List one or two specific ways that each priority could be expressed in your life right now.

For example, if you list your family among your top daily priorities, you might decide to express that priority by developing the habit of asking questions and listening attentively in each of the relationships involved.

It is crucial to remember that we can't practice all our daily priorities all the time. In our effort to be "good Christians," we often become burned-out believers. God wants us to focus on our top priorities—which may change over the years—and fit the others around them, adjusting to the demands of life. God honors this kind of faithfulness. Understanding our priorities biblically will also help us when we find new blocks of free time and we want to decide how to use that time wisely.

d. Put a check mark beside those daily priorities listed on pages 42-43, that you feel are operating properly in your life.

6. Time pressure can lead to poor decisions. One way to tell if that is happening is to examine the quality of the attention your lifelong priorities are getting.

a. For each priority you listed for question 5a, ask yourself, Am I allowing time pressure to cause me to make choices that significantly limit the expression of this priority in my life? If so, how?

b. Brainstorm on how you could change your use of time to be able to give attention to those lifelong priorities that are being neglected.

7. What are some things that can blur your view of God's
perspective and your priorities?

    a. Luke 8:14

    How might these things affect your use of time?

    b. 1 Thessalonians 2:4

    What pressure would this factor put on your priorities
    and time?

    c. James 1:22-24

How might James have advised you to apply this to your schedules?

d. Philippians 2:21

How would this factor influence what you "make" time for?

8. We can become so busy and/or preoccupied—even with "religious" things—that the plans and people God has for our todays become interruptions and annoyances.

What principles and attitudes that you discover in the following verses could help as you work at the tough job of managing your time well?

Psalm 90:12

Proverbs 16:9

Proverbs 21:5

Philippians 3:13-14

Matthew 25:21

9. As you try to sort out the maze of demands, opportunities, and commitments concerning your time, of what can you be assured?

    a. Psalm 139:16

How could knowing this help in the midst of pressure?

    b. Psalm 143:8,10

In what practical way(s) could you depend on God for this?

    c. Matthew 11:28

What do you think Jesus means by this?

10. a. Look over questions 1-9. How is God challenging and encouraging you concerning

your attitude toward time?

your use of time?

b. How can you begin to respond practically to that challenge this week?

Remember the replacement principle: If you're planning to add something to your schedule, you may need to take something out, or reduce the time you give to it.

Teach me, O LORD, to follow your decrees;
then I will keep them to the end.
(Psalm 119:33)

CHAPTER FIVE

RELATIONSHIPS

We live in an era of tense relationships. From casual acquaintances and business associates to the intimacy of close friendship and marriage, relationships are besieged with pressure. Some of it comes from outside the relationship; most of the pressure results from the dynamics *within* the relationship or the individuals involved.

Our relationships will never, in this life, be completely free from tension. Therefore, God is concerned that we increasingly understand and handle these relational stresses in ways that reflect His Person and His purpose.

CONTRIBUTING FACTORS

1. Proverbs is rich with practical wisdom. It pinpoints many attitudes and behaviors that significantly affect our relationships.

a. Examine the following verses in Proverbs and list the attitudes and/or behavior described.

11:3

11:13

11:25

12:18

15:1

17:9

29:22

b. Some of the things you listed are "pressure-producers," while others are "pressure-relievers." Put a check mark beside the traits you feel are consistently true of you.

2. James was deeply concerned about the relational tensions that existed among those to whom he wrote. He was painfully straightforward in addressing the issue. Read James 3:14-16 and James 4:1-3.

a. What does James identify as the source of the friction?

b. We may often struggle with the same tendency. Most often it appears in small ways, in ordinary issues. These small irritations wear away the peace in a relationship.

List two or three ways that selfishness can produce tension in your relationships.

3. Proverbs 13:10 describes another major source of tension in relationships.

    a. What is it?

    b. How can you tell if this factor is a *major* contributor to some pressure you experience in a relationship?

4. If we increasingly practice what is described in Philippians 2:3-8, we will gradually reduce our proud and selfish behavior in relationships.

    a. What attitudes and actions do you discover in this passage? List them on the chart. Then think of one or two specific ways you could apply each attitude and action in your relationships.

ATTITUDE OR ACTION	POSSIBLE APPLICATION
Be humble toward others, treat them with respect.	Say "please" and "thank you," especially to my children and those who work for me.

b. Do you think one of the applications would be helpful in a relationship of yours that is presently strained? If so, how and when could you begin to implement it?

RELATING BIBLICALLY TO OTHERS

Life can be so fast paced that we don't stop long enough to deal properly with the issues that create pressure in our relationships. The next two passages describe situations that took *time* and *effort* to resolve.

5. Read Daniel 1:8-14.

a. How did Daniel and the chief official differ on the issue that came up in Daniel's training?

b. What did Daniel do to resolve the problem?

c. How did the chief official respond?

d. Summarize the principle Daniel took the time to apply in his dilemma. First Corinthians 1:10 talks about the same principle.

6. Read Acts 11:1-18.

    a. Describe the situation.

    b. In order to handle the encounter the way he did, what attitude do you think Peter had?

    c. What do you think was the attitude of Peter's listeners?

    d. Compare Acts 11:1-18 with Proverbs 4:7 and James 1:19. What principle worked to make the incident in Acts 11 pleasing to God?

7. Philippians 4:2-3 describes tension in a relationship. The principles in questions 5 and 6 were needed to reconcile the individuals involved.

    a. What practical steps would have helped the two people carry out those principles?

b. If you need to apply one or both of these principles to a relationship of yours that is currently under pressure, what step can you take to get started?

8. Unreasonable or inappropriate expectations can be a source of inordinate pressure in any relationship. (Reasonable, appropriate expectations create pressures, too. Those pressures can be handled best using the principles that apply to responsibilities. Refer to chapter 6.)

a. How would you describe an unreasonable or inappropriate expectation?

b. What principles should you apply as you place expectations on others?

Mark 10:45

Colossians 2:2-3

Colossians 3:13-14

1 Thessalonians 2:10-12

1 Thessalonians 5:14

c. What understanding do the following verses give you about responding biblically when unreasonable expectations are placed on you?

Romans 12:21

Galatians 5:1

1 Thessalonians 2:6

2 Timothy 1:7

d. How do you think Titus 3:1-2 works together with the verses in part c?

e. When the expectations of others are crushing, and your options are limited, what encouragement and applications can you draw from the following verses?

Psalm 34:18

Psalm 68:19

Isaiah 57:15

1 Peter 2:19

1 Peter 2:23

9. Many of us experience the pressure that results from the involvement of a third party in a relationship. This pressure can take several forms:

a. You want to please two people, yet their differing expectations make that difficult.

b. One person is trying very hard to influence you concerning the other (either negatively or positively).

c. A third person is trying to intervene in order to help the primary relationship in some way.

Choose one of the three circumstances above. (If you identify strongly with one, choose it.) Using what you've learned in questions 1-8, decide which principle would contribute to handling the situation wisely. What practical step could help you put that principle into action in the relationship?

10. Look over questions 1-9.

a. How has God encouraged you?

b. Has God instructed you about current or potential pressure in a relationship?

If so, describe the pressure and what you will do to begin to apply His perspective?

If not, identify one attitude that you can develop or change in order to better apply God's perspective to future relational pressures. What step can you take to get started?

You may find this outline helpful as you try to be specific and practical in applying God's perspective to your relationships or to any other aspect of your life.

Issue: the issue God addresses Himself to, and what needs to occur in response to His perspective

Passage: any scripture God uses to bring the issue to your attention and express His perspective on the issue

Principle: the principle from those scriptures that applies to your situation

Plan: one or two specific steps you will take to apply God's perspective to the issue. Keep these small and realistic. Be careful not to express *intention* ("I'll try harder to understand"). Express *action* ("I will ask Craig why he did that, and I'll listen to his answer").

Let us therefore make every effort
to do what leads to peace
and to mutual edification.
(Romans 14:19)

CHAPTER SIX

RESPONSIBILITIES

We often sense the weight of pressure as we carry out our responsibilities. So much seems to depend on us, and sometimes our responsibilities seem to be so much larger than our ability to carry them out. God wants us to see our everyday responsibilities with His eyes, so that in attitude and in choice we can commit ourselves enthusiastically to what He gives us to do.

1. Describe the responsibilities of the following people. Think of at least one pressure that comes with each responsibility.

RESPONSIBILITY	POSSIBLE PRESSURE
Aaron (Exodus 28:4,29-30)	
Parents (Deuteronomy 6:5-7)	

RESPONSIBILITY	POSSIBLE PRESSURE
District Officers (1 Kings 4:22-23,26-28)	
Timothy (1 Timothy 4:11-14)	

2. Joshua 7:1-12 and 1 Samuel 17:4-7,26,32,34-37, and 45-47 depict two battle scenes.

a. Study each one based on the categories below.

	JOSHUA	1 SAMUEL
Difficulty of the task		
Action taken		
Results		

b. How did David's view of God differ from that of the Israelites at Ai? Use details from the passage to support your answer.

c. Based on this comparison, what do you think is essential in influencing the outcome of a situation?

3. As we carry out our responsibilities, God looks through the effort, with its success or failure, to our hearts.

   a. Examine the scriptures that follow and determine the foundational beliefs and attitudes you need to develop in order to face your responsibilities in a way that pleases God. Also identify what might be the opposite attitudes (often unconscious) in each instance.

BELIEF OR ATTITUDE	OPPOSITE
1 Samuel 2:6-9 It all depends on God.	It all depends on me.
Psalm 18:29,32	

BELIEF OR ATTITUDE	OPPOSITE
Ecclesiastes 8:15	
Ephesians 6:7-8	

b. The opposite beliefs and attitudes you listed are often the source of needless pressure. In the chart below, copy each opposite you listed in part a. Then suggest one or two pressures that each belief or attitude might create as you try to carry out your responsibilities.

OPPOSITES	POSSIBLE PRESSURE
It all depends on me.	I take on too much. I refuse to delegate or ask for help. I make myself indispensable.

c. Reflect on your responsibilities. Then, in parts a and b, underline any beliefs, attitudes, and pressures you identify with.

Optional
Examine 2 Chronicles 16:7-9. Describe what God is looking for and what He will do as He interacts with us in our responsibilities.

---

4. Our beliefs undergird the way we carry out our responsibilities, and directly influence the results of our efforts.

a. In Jeremiah 17:5-8, a curse and a blessing are contrasted. Use the chart below to record your observations.

BELIEFS	RESULTS
A curse (verses 5-6)	
A blessing (verses 7-8)	

b. What are some other results you can expect as you increasingly line up your attitudes to please God?

Ecclesiastes 3:12-13

Isaiah 26:3, Romans 8:6

1 John 3:21-22

5. Beliefs and attitudes *ground* us in our responsiblities. Choices and actions *move us forward* in God's strength.

a. What do the following verses reveal about how you are to carry out your responsibilities?

Leviticus 19:36

2 Chronicles 29:11

2 Chronicles 31:21

Psalm 78:72

1 Timothy 4:15

James 3:13

b. Based on your discoveries in part a, how would you counsel someone who is experiencing pressure because he or she is *not* carrying out a responsibility well?

6. Authority over other people comes with responsibility. That authority takes different outward forms in the home, in the work place, and in the community. Exercising our authority properly is an integral part of being responsible.

a. Read Matthew 20:25-28 and 1 Peter 5:3. In your exercise of authority, what are you to avoid?

b. Imagine you have the opportunity to advise a friend on how to firmly exercise the authority that is part of his or her responsibility. You want to encourage biblical attitudes and behavior, and discourage the misuse of authority. Look over questions 1 and 8a in chapter 5 and questions 2-6a in this chapter. Then list at least three specific pieces of advice you would give, based on what you've learned.

c. Does any of your biblical advice apply to a situation in which you have some authority? If so, how?

7. Read the parable Jesus told about the talents (coins) as it's recorded in Matthew 25:14-30.

a. The first two servants received different numbers of talents. Why, then, do you think they received the same enthusiastic praise from their master?

b. Why did the third servant get a different response?

c. If you had been there to interview that master, what traits do you think he would have chosen to describe a good servant?

8. Jethro, Moses' father-in-law, observed that Moses had allowed a responsibility to turn into a nightmare. We can experience the same problem. Read Exodus 18:13-26.

a. How did Jethro describe the problem?

b. What did Jethro say would result if no change took place?

c. What change was needed?

d. What does this incident teach you about what can happen when a God-given responsibility overgrows its bounds?

e. How can you tell if you have allowed any of your responsibilities to grow out of proportion to God's intentions?

9. a. Write a list of your responsibilities below. Be inclusive; that is, include things like coaching a sports team and volunteering at school, in addition to your major responsibilities.

*	RESPONSIBILITY	P	O

b. Review the priorities you determined you should have in chapter 4, question 5. Put an * to the left of your responsibilities that reflect those priorities.

c. Mark a P to the right of any responsibilities that are a source of significant pressure to you. (Remember that you can feel pressure from *not* fulfilling a responsibility as much as from trying to fulfill it.) Mark an O to the right of any responsibilities that have overgrown their bounds. (This process takes thought, honesty, and courage.)

10. a. Look over questions 1-9. As God looks at your responsibilities, what change do you think He would like to see you make?

b. What scripture in this chapter clarifies, challenges, and/or encourages you concerning the change described above?

c. List one or two steps you will take to begin to make that change. Be specific; for instance, "I'll call Bill and tell him I won't be running the program after this term is up."

This is the point at which intention and understanding are translated into choice. It can be a painful process, but God greatly rewards it.

> *This is what the LORD says—*
>   *your Redeemer, the Holy One of Israel:*
> *"I am the Lord your God,*
>   *who teaches you what is best for you,*
>   *who directs you in the way you should go.*
> *If only you had paid attention to my commands,*
>   *your peace would have been like a river,*
>   *your righteousness like the waves of the sea."*
>
>   (Isaiah 48:17-18)

CHAPTER SEVEN

FINANCES

We would be hard-pressed to find an adult today who has not experienced significant financial pressure. That pressure doesn't necessarily arise from a lack of money (although, of course, it often does); sometimes it comes from issues of choice and/or attitude.

As we face our own financial stresses, God desires that we adopt His perspective and act according to His Word. In doing so, we'll be able to avoid some financial pressures altogether, and we'll learn how to deal biblically with the ones that do become part of our experience.

1. First Chronicles 29 records words of praise that David prayed near the end of his life. His prayer is a grand yet simple summary of what he believed about God. Read verses 10-14.

    a. Write down one or two observations about David's beliefs concerning how God relates to wealth and possessions.

b. With these beliefs, what attitudes do you think David had

in times of prosperity?

in times of want?

2. Psalm 17:15, Psalm 19:14, and Psalm 27:8 give us a glimpse of the predominant concerns of David's life. A careful reading of those verses will help you answer the following questions.

a. How do you think David's predominant concerns affected

his desire for money and things?

his management of what God provided?

b. How would those concerns help explain David's response in Psalm 4:1,7-8?

3. What do the following verses reveal about the significance of money and possessions?

Psalm 39:5-6

Psalm 49:7-9

Psalm 119:72

4. Attitudes can create or contribute to pressure in financial circumstances. These attitudes can exist among the rich, the poor, and everyone in between. Discover some of these attitudes in the following verses:

a. Proverbs 15:27

How might the family of this man experience trouble?

b. 1 Timothy 6:9-10

What "traps" do you think someone with this attitude might fall into? What pressures would result?

5. Financial increase and financial decrease bring potential pressures (for both the righteous and the unrighteous). Being aware of these potential pressures is the first step in managing them wisely.

a. Of what possible tendencies should we be aware when finances are increasing?

Deuteronomy 8:10-18

Psalm 62:10

Ecclesiastes 5:10

James 5:3,5

b. What pressures may accompany financial decrease?

Nehemiah 5:4-5

Proverbs 19:7

Proverbs 30:8-9

Matthew 6:31-32

Can you think of other pressures?

c. In a and b, underline any pressures you identify with from past or present experience.

d. If you viewed your pressures from David's perspective (questions 1 and 2), would your responses be (or have been) different? If so, how?

Optional
Compare 2 Kings 4:1-7 and Mark 8:1-8. Try to write a statement
about how God relates available resources to needs.

6. Financial distress can come upon us through no fault of
our own. On the other hand, we can bring problems on ourselves as a result of our choices and patterns.

What choices and patterns (wise and unwise) are described in the following verses? What beliefs might these
choices and patterns stem from? How can they show up in
actions or habits?

CHOICE OR PATTERN	ACTION OR HABIT
Proverbs 13:15 *Lack of faithfulness.*	*Late for work. Doesn't keep commitments. Doesn't finish what he starts.*
Proverbs 14:23	
Proverbs 22:26-27	

7. Whether your financial stress is beyond your control or within your control, what choices, principles, and attitudes described in the following verses will help relieve the pressure?

    a. Proverbs 11:24, 19:17

    What could this choice prevent?

    b. Proverbs 13:11

    What habit might be based on this principle?

    c. Proverbs 23:4

    How can you tell if you are applying this verse?

    d. Isaiah 25:1,4

    How could this truth help during financial stress?

    e. Romans 13:7-8

    What financial "rule of thumb" could you formulate from this passage?

8. What principles do you discover in the following passages that can help you relate biblically to the ups and downs of your financial life? Do your best to be clear enough so that you could share the principles with a friend for whom they would be helpful.

Ecclesiastes 5:18-20

Philippians 4:12, 1 Timothy 6:6-8

9. Based on your study in questions 1-8, how would you respond to one or two of the following statements? Include some of the Bible references that contribute to your thinking. (There is no one right answer; your honest, thoughtful integration of God's perspective with the realities of life will take you in the right direction.)

    a. "Our expenses exceed our income."

    b. "We don't have enough money to be able to give to others."

    c. "I don't have financial worries. I have enough money to last me a long, long time."

    d. "It would take me forever to get out of debt."

    e. "I am often anxious about our finances."

10. a. Describe any financial pressures you are facing right now related to the state or the management of your finances.

b. As you looked at God's perspective through the scriptures in this study, what did you discover about

any attitudes, actions, or habits on your part that may be contributing to your pressure?

any attitudes, actions, or habits that would help relieve and/or manage the pressure?

an attitude or a habit you can develop that will help prevent or manage some future financial pressure?

c. What can you do this week to begin to implement
what you learned? Is there

a choice you can make?
a change you can launch?
a verse you can memorize?
a sin you need to confess?
a habit you can begin?
a habit you can break?

You may want to use the IPPP outline on page 57.

May the God of peace . . .
equip you with everything good
for doing his will,
and may he work in us
what is pleasing to him,
through Jesus Christ,
to whom be glory for ever and ever.
(Hebrews 13:20-21)

CHAPTER EIGHT

OUR CALLING

Because we have responded to God, through faith in Christ, the Apostle Paul calls us "new creations" (2 Corinthians 5:17). In this new life we face unique pressures—pressures that will not be experienced by those who have not committed their lives to Christ. We are to try to understand and prepare for these pressures.

1. In every area of our existence, living the Christian life bears the element of pressure.

 a. As you examine the following verses, try to determine *why* it is that living obediently to Christ is an endeavor laced with pressure. Can you give an everyday example that illustrates each reason?

REASON	EXAMPLE
Romans 7:21-23, Galatians 5:16-17	

REASON	EXAMPLE
Ephesians 6:12	
1 John 2:15-16	

b. Are you currently experiencing pressure for one of these reasons? If so, what is the reason?

2. Paul had no illusions about the difficulty of interacting with these sources of pressure. He described it as warfare (Ephesians 6:10-18). The Apostle Peter asserted that we are fighting to protect our souls (1 Peter 2:11). State several facts about our warfare (one is listed already). Such a list will serve as a reminder of the seriousness of being prepared for facing these pressures.

Warfare requires weapons

3. Read John 17:13-18.

    a. List some of the statements Jesus made about His disciples' interaction with Him and with the world in which they lived.

    b. Because you are "in the world" but not "of the world," what pressures do you think will characterize your life?

    c. Jesus was criticized for His association with sinners (Matthew 9:11). Using John 17:15 and 18 as your base, compare 1 Corinthians 5:9-11 and 1 Peter 1:15. What observations do you make concerning

    your involvement with people?

    your moral standards?

    the tensions involved in living these truths?

    d. How would you respond to those Christians who deal with these pressures by separating themselves, as much as possible, from the world?

4. The pressures of being "in the world" but not "of" it will bear down on us.

    a. How are we told to live?

    Luke 11:28

    1 Timothy 6:11

    2 Timothy 2:3

    1 Peter 1:13,5:8

    b. What are some *attitudes* we need to keep developing in order to live increasingly the way we are told?

    Psalm 25:1-2

    Psalm 138:8

    Habakkuk 3:17-18

    2 Corinthians 4:5

    1 Peter 4:12-13,16

c. The very pressures themselves help us live as we should. What does Romans 5:3-4 help us understand about that?

5. Paul suffered many agonies as he lived out his calling in a hostile world. Read 2 Corinthians 1:8 and 2 Corinthians 11:24-29 for a glimpse of the pressures he experienced.

Now imagine you are with the apostle, and in answer to your questions, he speaks the words of 2 Corinthians 1:9-11 and 2 Corinthians 4:1,7-12.

a. Try to summarize what Paul asserts that God is accomplishing through the incredible stress.

b. Paul describes his driving concern in Philippians 3:8-10. What effect do you think this aim had on how he viewed the pressure he experienced?

6. Compromise is an enemy of our intention to follow God. The pressure to compromise is stronger in some areas than in others, and we are all different in our strengths and weaknesses.

a. The verses on page 86 depict some common areas of compromise. Identify each area. Then, on the right, list a circumstance of your life that has the *potential* to create pressure to compromise. This is difficult to do because it forces us to face our own potential to fail and/or sin. But honesty and deliberate clarity will help us to "be careful," as we are told to do in 2 Corinthians 10:12:

*"So if you think you are standing firm,
be careful that you don't fall."*

AREA OF COMPROMISE	YOUR CIRCUMSTANCE
Proverbs 12:22	
1 Corinthians 6:18	
1 Corinthians 14:20, 2 Peter 3:1	
Philippians 2:4,21	

b. Is there an area not mentioned above in which you experience the pressure to compromise? If so, what is it?

c. What circumstances and/or attitudes contribute to the pressure?

d. Examine 2 Timothy 3:16-17 and Hebrews 4:12. In what ways can God's Word help you when you sense pressure to compromise?

7. What are some evidences that begin to appear when we consistently give in to pressure and fail to persevere?

Isaiah 29:13

1 Corinthians 3:1-3

Revelation 3:15

8. As we walk through life, we need strengthening. We need support. We need help.

a. How does God strengthen and support us?

Psalm 119:28

John 16:24

Romans 8:31-39

Ephesians 3:16

2 Peter 1:3-8

b. What are some ways we are to cooperate with God in that strengthening? How might that cooperation be demonstrated in our habits, activities, and behavior?

WAYS TO COOPERATE	HABIT/ACTIVITY/BEHAVIOR
Psalm 119:9,104,133	
2 Corinthians 10:5	
Colossians 3:2	
Hebrews 4:16	

c. How can we, as Christians, help and strengthen one another?

Romans 15:7

Romans 15:30

Colossians 3:16

1 Peter 1:22

1 Peter 4:10

Put a check mark beside the kinds of support you feel that you need right now. To whom could you go for such support?

Put an O beside the kinds of help you feel you can offer others. Is there someone who needs your strengthening help? If so, what can you do to give it?

9. In the midst of telling His disciples what they would face as they lived for Him, Jesus provided them with the ultimate assurance of victory. Read John 16:33.

a. How do you think this assurance helped the disciples face the pressures ahead with God's perspective?

b. How can it help you face the pressure you identified in question 1b?

10. Look over questions 1-9.

a. What new understanding have you gained concerning the pressures involved in following Christ?

b. What issue(s) in your own life has God spoken to? Identify a verse or passage that gives you God's perspective on this issue.

c. What will you begin to do, or change, in order to bring this issue in line with God's perspective?

Not that I have already obtained all this,
or have already been made perfect,
but I press on to take hold of that
for which Christ Jesus took hold of me.
(Philippians 3:12)

Suggestions for Study Group Leaders

1. Read "Before You Begin" together (pages 7-8), emphasizing

    a. the opportunity to develop in biblical thinking.

    b. the opportunity to become personal and practical in applying God's Word.

    c. the nature of the study which allows a broad range of answers to many questions. (Many people become frustrated when they can't put things in neat packages; you will need to help them focus on the *process* of learning, rather than the *product* of "right" answers.)

2. The first three chapters are crucial: they deal with developing a biblical thinking process concerning pressure. That thinking process is the foundation needed to examine the topics of the last five chapters. Make sure that everyone in your group completes those initial three chapters.

3. Set the example for faithful preparation and personal application.

4. As you create discussion questions,

- Try to ask questions that require a thoughtful interaction with both the *information* discovered and the *understanding* it provides.

- Center your questions around God's Word and the students' response to it. Try to avoid discussions that revolve around opinions only.

- Encourage specific responses concerning the personal application of God's Word. You might want to leave a healthy slice of the group time to spend on those personal questions in the study.

5. You may choose to lead the discussion by going through one question at a time. (Be careful to plan your time and move from one question to the next when you need to.) With this method, members of the group can take turns leading.

6. Pray for the individuals in your group. Be sensitive to those who may need drawing out, but don't force participation. Ask God's Spirit to stimulate the dynamic of mutual ministry within the group.

7. If you, the leader, desire to do extra study, consider these ideas:

- Choose one or more key words or concepts in the chapter. Using a complete concordance, trace and study the words (or words related to the concept) through the Scriptures, or through the New Testament.

- Zero in on one of the passages in the study. Ask yourself more questions about the passage (why, how, etc.). Find another passage, or several verses, on the same theme. Combine the aspects of truth into a summary.

- Choose one or more principles you discovered as you studied. Examine the Scriptures for situations that demonstrate the principle.

8. Remember that you are a guide and God is the Teacher. Acknowledging this fact will help you relax and enjoy your role, knowing that each student's personal adventure is not dependent on your ability to teach or lead.

9. You may find a book such as *How to Lead Small Groups* by Neal F. McBride (NavPress) helpful as you seek to broaden your leadership skills.

SMALL-GROUP MATERIALS FROM NAVPRESS

BIBLE STUDY SERIES

DESIGN FOR DISCIPLESHIP
GOD IN YOU
GOD'S DESIGN FOR THE FAMILY
INSTITUTE OF BIBLICAL
  COUNSELING SERIES

LEARNING TO LOVE SERIES
LIFECHANGE
LOVE ONE ANOTHER
STUDIES IN CHRISTIAN LIVING
THINKING THROUGH DISCIPLESHIP

TOPICAL BIBLE STUDIES

Becoming a Woman of
  Excellence
Becoming a Woman of Freedom
Becoming a Woman of Purpose
The Blessing Study Guide
Celebrating Life
Growing in Christ
Growing Strong in God's Family
Homemaking
Intimacy with God

Loving Your Husband
Loving Your Wife
A Mother's Legacy
Strategies for a Successful
  Marriage
Surviving Life in the Fast Lane
To Run and Not Grow Tired
To Walk and Not Grow Weary
What God Does When Men Pray
When the Squeeze Is On

BIBLE STUDIES WITH COMPANION BOOKS

Bold Love
The Feminine Journey
From Bondage to Bonding
Hiding from Love
Inside Out
The Masculine Journey
The Practice of Godliness
The Pursuit of Holiness

Secret Longings of the
  Heart
Spiritual Disciplines
Tame Your Fears
Transforming Grace
Trusting God
What Makes a Man?
The Wounded Heart
Your Work Matters to God

RESOURCES

Brothers!
How to Lead Small Groups
Jesus Cares for Women
The Small Group Leaders
  Training Course

Topical Memory System (KJV/NIV
  and NASB/NKJV)
Topical Memory System: Life
  Issues (KJV/NIV and
  NASB/NKJV)

VIDEO PACKAGES

Bold Love
Hope Has Its Reasons
Inside Out
Living Proof

Parenting Adolescents
Unlocking Your Sixth Suitcase
Your Home, A Lighthouse